Dear girlfriend,

God is so good. Just knowing you has been one of my greatest blessings. The more I get to know you, the more I am thankful. God bless you this birthday and give you a great year of and with so many blessings.

Love,
Everman

GOD IS!

MARK R. LITTLETON

STARBURST  PUBLISHERS

P. O. Box 4123, Lancaster, Pennsylvania 17604

To schedule Author appearances write: Author Appearances, Starburst Promotions, P.O. Box 4123, Lancaster, Pennsylvania 17604 or call (717) 293-0939.

Credits:
Cover by David Marty Design
Illustrations by Bill Dussinger

Unless otherwise noted, or paraphrased by the author, all Scripture quotations are from the King James Version of The Holy Bible.

We, the Publisher and Authors, declare that to the best of our knowledge all material (quoted or not) contained herein is accurate, and we shall not be held liable for the same.

First Printing, April 1997
ISBN: 0-914984-926
Library of Congress Catalog Number 96-072293
Printed in the United States of America.

Table of Contents

God is Love!

*The one who does not love,
does not know God,
for God is love.*

—*1 John 4:8* NASB

God Is!

*H*ow great is God's love?

F. B. Meyer said,
"It's like the Amazon River flowing down
to water one daisy."
The Amazon is a river, though,
while God's love
can never fail,
can never run dry,
can never go bad, and
can never cease
to water each of us
wherever we are
today and forever.

God Is!

*I read about a little boy watching
his mom peel the outer layers
of an onion. He said,
"Is that paper, Mom?"
"No," she explained,
"It's a special covering to keep
the insides safe.
Many things have a covering
like that. Even we do."
She was referring,
of course, to our skin.
The little boy answered reverently,
"I know: God's love."*

God Is!

I always liked that story of the little girl who was drawing away one day in Sunday School as if she planned to add her artwork to the ceiling of the Sistine Chapel. Asked what she was sketching, she said, "God." "But no one knows what God looks like," her teacher protested, undoubtedly thinking she should correct this "heresy." The little girl just smiled cryptically. "They will when I'm done."

God Is!

"*For God so loved the world,
that He gave His only begotten Son,
that whoever believes in Him should not
perish, but have everlasting life.*"
Every Sunday School kid knows that verse.
But what does it tell us?
Four things God can't do:
He can't love us more than
He has loved us.
He can't give more than He has given.
He can't make the way to salvation simpler.
He can't offer us any greater gift.
We might think there is nothing
God can't do. But it's not true.
In Christ, He gave us everything
that mattered to Him.
He simply couldn't do anymore for us
and still be God.

*W*hat does God tell us when we suffer?
Three things:
"I know. I care.
I will walk with you through it."

God Is!

God's love is what drives
Him to seek us even when we hide,
to give us rain and life and
refreshment even when we run,
to extend to us a hand as we struggle
in the mire even when we doubt.
God's love is so great that
He won't give up on us
even when we've given up on Him.

God Is!

The love of God shone
on me one morning. At 3 a.m.,
my then five-year old daughter
tottered into my bedroom.
In the dim glow of the night light she looked
disheveled, disarming, a waif.
Trembling. Shivering.
"Daddy, can I sleep in your bed?"
"It's three o'clock, honey."
"I heard a noise. I'm scared."
"There's nothing to be scared of."
"I know. But I am. Please, Daddy."
I well remembered those days
when I was five and strange sounds
in the night whispered to me that some
beast lay under my bed waiting
for just the right moment to pounce.
My heart would thud.

God Is!

I would huddle under the blankets,
thinking they would protect me,
desperately praying
it would go away.
I gazed into Alisha's pleading eyes,
then opened the covers.
"Okay, hop in." I sighed,
rolled over and was just about asleep
when I felt two arms around my neck.
"I love you, Daddy."
A kiss on the cheek.
Tiny, soft lips.
I murmured,
"I love you too, honey. Now go to sleep."
She curled up, a little hump at my back.
The next morning I found her there,
cuddled up and breathing securely.
I smiled and said,
"Thanks for the little love pat, Lord."

thirteen

God Is!

"*God is love.*" *What does it mean?*
If God were only just, He'd punish
us each the moment we sinned.
If God were only holy,
He'd abhor us so much that
He never would have brought us
into existence in the first place.
If God were only gracious,
He'd spoil us into boredom.
If He were only all-powerful,
He would try to stun us with displays that
would probably scare us into hiding.
If God were only . . .
Forget the "onlys."
God Is all these things.
It's when He is all these things at once that
He is love.

God Is!

How high is God's love?
Higher than the heavens;
it covers all of you.
How deep is God's love?
Unfathomable, says scripture;
it has no bottom,
yet it's close enough
to catch you when you fall.
How wide is God's love?
As far as the east is from west,
yet small enough to hug you hard
and long and keep an arm over your shoulder
as you walk down a dark street.
How long is God's love?
Long enough to keep you safe
from life to death
and back into life again . . . forever.

God Is!

People sometimes ask,
"Where is God's love?
How has He loved us?
How has He loved me?"
In a railroad accident, a number
of people were killed,
including a boy of only ten.
The distraught father stumbled
about in despair, crying,
"Where was God when my boy died?"
An old conductor, a survivor of the wreck,
stopped the man and said,
"I suppose God was in the same place He was when
His own Son died on the cross."
For a moment, both sets of eyes met and then
together they embraced and consoled one another,
the one assuring the other that because of what
Christ did on that cross he would see his son again.

sixteen

God Is!

When troubles enter our lives,
we often wonder if God's love has failed,
or if He has ceased to love us.
Scripture says His love never fails,
and that He would never desert or forsake us.
Thus, we must find some other explanation.
An old preacher once told me,
"It is God's love that allows troubles to come;
it is God's love that strengthens us in them;
and it is God's love that gets us past them.
God never said He would take
us out of our difficulties and distresses,
or that He would take them all out of our lives.
No, He only promises that
when problems come,
He will go with us through them."

God Is!

One day I asked God why
He loved me.
He seemed to say, "Because."
"But why?" I pressed.
"Because I chose to," He said.
It felt cold.
"But why did you choose to?"
"Because of who I am," He said.
It felt distant. I wanted something more.
"Was it because of who I was?"
"No," He answered.
"You were lost, a sinner, disgraced.
There was nothing to commend you to Me."
I was aghast. "Then was it because of who
I would become?"
"No," He said.
"I have made you all you are."
I felt humbled. Finally I said,

God Is!

"But why, Lord?
There must be some reason
why you loved me."
"There was," He said.
"Before you ever were, I knew you.
Before you had ever done
anything right or wrong,
I wanted you for My own.
Before you had any potential,
before anyone else saw in you
a glimmer of greatness or even goodness,
I saw you as a helpless child,
and I loved you."
I was amazed. "So you have always loved me?"
"And I always will."
I laughed for joy, it felt so good.
I said, "Then I don't have anything
to worry about." This time He laughed.
"That's what I've been trying to tell you!"

God Is!

Ultimately, the greatest picture
of God's love is the cross.
Jesus nailed there.
His whole body on fire.
His soul in hell. Naked. Ridiculed.
Soldiers gambling for His clothing.
The crowd hurling insults.
And the Father Himself channeling wrath at
Him in one spirit-wrenching blast.
Taking the blame for us.
Sacrificing Himself that we might live.
We've heard it so many times,
it loses its power.
That's why God gave the Jews Passover.
A lamb from the flock was brought into the
home and stayed for a whole week.
The kids played with it.
The parents laughed as it gamboled about,

God Is!

cute, precious, funny, adorable.
So eager. So innocent.
Maybe the kids even taught
it some tricks and named it.
"Mama, watch this.
Look at what I taught Jester."
Or "Curlie." Or, "Jo."
But Mama bites her lip. She knows what's coming.
On Friday afternoon everything changes.
Dad takes the lamb outside. He has a knife and a
rope and a grim look in his eyes.
The kids start crying.
Mama asks why they have to do this now.
The lamb prances and jerks about
on the rope, excited.
What's happening now?
What's this new thing they're doing?
The lamb thinks this is just one more wondrous
moment in a week of wondrous moments.

God Is!

Papa ties up the lamb.
He lifts the knife.
The family watches. Waits. Cringes.
Cries. With one deft motion,
Papa cuts the lamb's throat.
It's that brutal.
Jewish kids never forget that moment.
They tried not to love the lamb the next year.
They said they wouldn't care.
But they couldn't help it.
The lamb was just too innocent.
Too perfect. Too eager and frolicking and fun.
Every year they fell in love with the lamb,
and every year they watched him die.
As some watched Jesus that day on Golgotha,
they must have remembered the Passover
lambs of their youth.
Innocent. Gentle. Adorable. Lovable.
Dying like that . . . that they might live.

God Is!

A Sunday School teacher
counseled me one Sunday.
I feared God might stop loving me,
or give up on me or cast me out just for spite.
The teacher said,
"The Bible teaches God's love is eternal;
so it can never end, right?"
I nodded. "It teaches God's love is infinite;
so it will never run out. Correct?"
"I guess," I said. He went on,
"God's love is immutable;
so it can never change.
And God's love is irresistible;
it can never fail. Do you understand?"
"I think."
He gazed at me, as if into my soul.
"If God's love is eternal, infinite,
immutable and irresistible,

God Is!

then the real question is:
"What have you and I got to
worry about?"
"Nothing," I said, the lights coming on.
"Correct," he said.
"Next subject."

"Take away love and our earth is a tomb."

—Robert Browning

God Is!

I tried to picture when Jesus agreed to go to the cross. Perhaps a conversation like this happened.

The Father:

"I need someone to save mankind."

Jesus: "I will go."

"It will mean the pains of hell."

"I will go."

"It will mean separation from Me."

"I will go."

"It will mean the pains of hell and separation from Me for the equivalent of eternity."

"I will still go."

The Father finally says, "But why?"

The conversation always ends this way:

"Because My love for them is far greater than any pain I might go through for them."

God Is!

*Karl Barth, the renowned theologian,
was once asked by reporters,
"What is the most profound theological
thought you've ever had?"
Barth thought a moment, then said,
"Jesus loves me, this I know,
for the Bible tells me so."
Indeed, that great children's
song contains not only our most
profound theological proposition,
but also our most mysterious.
Why me? Why us? Why anyone?*

God Is!

Sometimes I ask God,
"Why did You love me? Just me?"
I know He has loved all of us, equally,
infinitely. But why me? It seems that
He always gives me the same answer:
"Because I am love. And love has to love,
even the unlovable."
"So I'm unlovable?"
"At times!"
I knew then that He'd been talking to my wife.

God Is!

Many struggle with the idea of hell.
How could a God of perfect,
unlimited love send decent,
kind-hearted but unbelieving souls to hell?
The truth is God doesn't send anyone to hell.
When people reject Him and all He is,
they also reject all He has.
Hell becomes the only place left for them to go.
As C.S. Lewis said,
"There are those who say to Him,
'Thy will be done,' and those to whom He says,
'Thy will be done'."

God is All-Knowing!

LORD, *you have searched me and you know me.*
You know when I sit and when I rise;
you perceive my thoughts from afar.
You discern my going out and my lying down;
you are familiar with all my ways.
Before a word is on my tongue
you know it completely, O LORD . . .
Such knowledge is too wonderful
for me, too lofty for me to attain.

—Psalm 139:1-4,6 NIV

God is!

Knowledge is increasing at a tremendous pace. Some say mankind's collective knowledge about our world doubles every five years. Yet, the words of Thomas Edison, spoken in 1921, still stand: "We don't know the millionth part of one percent about anything. We don't know what water is. We don't know what light is. We don't know what gravitation is. We don't know what electricity is. We don't know what heat is. We have a lot of hypotheses about these things, but that is all." In contrast to our knowledge about our world, we possess tremendous knowledge of God. He has revealed to us everything we

God IS!

*need to know to walk with Him,
live right, succeed in life, invest in
the things that matter, reconcile broken
relationships, bring in world peace,
and live forever.
Amazingly, this knowledge has been available
for thousands of years, yet it is as up-to-date
as today's news.*

———•———

God IS!

*Some graffiti found on
a wall in a university bathroom said:
"God is dead."*

—Nietzsche

*Right below it:
"Nietzsche is dead."*

—God

God is!

God knows who we are, where
we are, what we're doing, and what
struggles we're facing every moment of
every day.
This can be scary, but also tremendously
liberating in a world where few of us
get our so-called "fifteen minutes of fame."
"To know that I am known and understood
— intimately, wholly, perfectly — at all times
and in all circumstances," said a friend,
"gives me true significance.
It proves that even if I matter to no one else,
I matter to God. God has made knowing me
His supreme passion." The Deists imagined a God
who wound up the universe like a clock,
then left it to unwind on its own without
God's involvement.
The God of the Bible is no such god.

God Is!

Our God is all-knowing, intimately
involved with every aspect of
His creation. Because of His
omniscience, we know we are seen,
understood, and loved so completely that
not a single atom of our nature and person
is overlooked. Truly, to Him,
we are the ultimate fascination
— as He should be to us.

———◆———

God IS!

*A school teacher assigned her first
grade students to write an essay on any
subject. One girl chose ants. She wrote,
"My subjek is 'Ants.' Ants is of two kinds,
insects and lady uncles. Sometimes they live in holes
and sometimes they crawl into the sugar bole,
and sometimes they live with their married sisters.
That is all I know about ants."
Ah, mankind.
For God, who knows each of us through
to our most inane thoughts and ideas,
it must be the ultimate form of fun.*

God IS!

Oh, the depth of the riches both of the
wisdom and knowledge of God!
How unsearchable are His judgments
and His ways past finding out!
For who has known the mind of the LORD?
Or who has become His counselor?
Or who has first given to Him
and it shall be repaid to him?
For of Him and through Him
and to Him are all things,
to whom be glory forever.
Amen.

—Romans 11:33-36 *NKJV*

God IS!

In this world, it's easy to think
no one notices us, no one cares.
Folks in nursing homes.
Single moms worked to the bone.
Dads who feel they've failed.
Pastors who despair because
their church hasn't grown in five years.
The homeless.
Not so with the all-knowing
Master of the universe.
It was like the concert my
daughter's school recently offered.
Alisha stood in the choir,
belted out her songs and smiled picturesquely.
When it was over, she ran up to us excited.
"Did you see me? Did you hear me?
Did you see how I kept my face smiling,
like the teacher told us to?" I assured her,

God IS!

"We saw all of it.
We even got pictures."
That especially thrilled her.
"When can I see them? When?"
In the same way, God has
"pictures," too, and treasures them.
One day He'll show them to all of us,
and we'll laugh and cry and rejoice together
in the knowledge of His "Daddylike" love.

———◆———

Mr. *Sparrow was a diabetic,
in his nineties, living in a nursing
home. A couple boarded him and his
wheelchair into their car each Sunday night
and brought him to our little service at church.
He would sit in his chair, bent over but belting
out hymns into his lap like he was the whole
baritone section of the choir.
When I visited him I almost always
found him praying — for the folks in the
nursing home, for his family, for our church.
He could laugh like wind through willows, and he
could weep like a man who has just lost everything.
I often marveled at his deep, committed spirituality.
One night as we dropped him off at the nursing
home after our church service, I said,
"Will they give you a snack before bed tonight,
Mr. Sparrow?" He replied, "No, the only snacks I*

get are talking to Jesus."
I laughed, but that was vintage
Mr. Sparrow: always a sage
little insight that would reorient my
thinking about God and prayer and
everything else.

God Is!

God has numbered the hairs on our
heads. That might seem like a dull thing to
record, but in reality, God doesn't count those
hairs the way we would. No, He simply knows.
Instantly. Effortlessly. Without investing time or motion.
At every moment of the day or month, the count is in
His mind. How? The same way you know two plus
two is four. It's instantaneous, complete, unerring knowledge.
Moreover, He knows not only the number of hairs,
but their lengths, widths, color, texture, where they fell out,
who (or what) picked them up, what the lady at the
beauty parlor did with them, in fact, their whole
personal histories. And He knows these things about
every atom of His creation. Cantaloupes, cats,
camels, capitals, continents . . . Everything!
No wonder David exclaimed,
"Such knowledge is too wonderful for me,
too lofty for me to attain!"

*Solomon Ibn Gabirol said, "There are four
mental types among human beings:
"The man who knows, and is aware that he knows;
he is wise, so inquire of him."
"The man who knows, but is unaware that he knows;
remind him and help him that he forget not."
"The man who is ignorant,
and knows that he is ignorant; teach him."
"The man who is ignorant, but pretends to know;
he is a fool,
so keep away from him."*

God knew us through to the heart
before we were ever conceived,
before anything in creation was created,
before we had done anything good or bad.
Scripture says He knew us, and loved us,
and died for us before we ever
exhibited the least interest in Him.
That is like a grandfather who puts
his grandchildren in his will and leaves them
everything they'll ever need
before they're even born.

God IS!

A father devised a game about
God that his kids could play while
they travel. On one occasion,
God's omniscience was the subject and
a conversation like this began
between the kids:
"God can hear all the automobile horns
in the world at the same time."
"Yeah, and what's more He knows the make
of the car behind each one. And its mileage."
"He knows how many people
in the world are bald."
"And whether it's in back, front, both,
or all over." "That's nothing. He can speak
every language without an accent."
"God knows every germ personally and
has a name for each one."
"God knows what would have happened

if we had done ten other things today
instead of this trip."
The talk went on and on with
each idea getting larger and larger,
until the man's wife sighed,
"When will we ever get there?"
"One thing for sure," Pop answered,
"God knows." And He does.

God IS!

Josh Billings said,
"The trouble with most folks isn't so
much their ignorance,
as knowing so many things that ain't so."
In contrast, God knows not only who
thinks things that "ain't so," but how to
move those folks in the direction of discovering
the things that are so.
And because He is also kind, compassionate,
loving and wise, He can accomplish this
without making them feel like idiots or fools,
even though others around them may think
that's exactly what they have become.

God IS!

*F*or You formed my inward parts;
You covered me in my mother's womb.
I will praise You, for I am fearfully and
wonderfully made; Marvelous are Your works,
And that my soul knows very well.
My frame was not hidden from You,
When I was made in secret,
And skillfully wrought
in the lowest parts of the earth.
Your eyes saw my substance,
being yet unformed.
And in Your book they all were written,
The days fashioned for me,
When as yet there were none of them.

—Psalm 139:13-16

God IS!

*P*eople on earth were angry.
They said God didn't understand.
They said He didn't know what
it was like to be oppressed, to be beaten,
to be rejected, to be hated.
They said He had no right to judge them,
or ask that they obey and trust Him.
God decided to make a deal.
"I will come among you and be one of you,"
He told them. "I will become a man."
"But you will come as a king," they complained.
"Few of us are kings and most are cruel."
"No," God answered, "I will come as a pauper,
the son of a laborer. I will work painstakingly
every day for my bread and water."
"Perhaps," the people said, "
but you will be a citizen, respected and protected."
"No," God told them, "I will be an outcast.

God is!

Some will spit upon me.
Many will hate me."
"But you will come as a healthy,
happy person with a great family, who has
nothing but good all his days,"
"No," God replied, "I will remain unmarried.
I will have no children, no legacy,
no one to call me Papa, no son to be proud of,
no daughter to praise.
I will know little more than sorrow all My days."
Some of the people were intrigued now,
but they said, "Then you will live long and well and
never know great physical pain."
God answered, "No, I will die a criminal's death,
at a young age." There was a long silence.
"Then," the people finally said, astonished,
"you will truly have been one of us and we can
gladly trust you. But when will you do this?"
God said, "I already have," and pointed to His Son.

God IS!

God knows every struggle we've had,
every burden we've borne,
every tragedy we've faced,
every mountain we've had to climb.
He knows all the choices we've made and why.
We need never fear being misunderstood by God,
or that any motive, situation or circumstance
will be overlooked.
He is in that sense the perfect Advocate.
We never need fear being judged by God
unfairly or superficially.
He will bring out every fact.
In this is great assurance, but also great fear.

God IS!

God's omniscience is not a cold,
calculating knowledge. It's wedded
to experience and understanding,
for He has been one of us. In Jesus He knows
what it's like to breathe dust, to face rejection, to
fight temptation. He has hurt in His soul because
His family and friends didn't understand Him.
He knows what it is to feel as if all has gone wrong and
our life is a failure and to wish for the easy way rather
than the hard way, then to choose the latter even though
everything in our body screams against it.
In Jesus, God has walked in our sandals.
He knows not only what it's like to be us,
but also how to help us become a little more like Him.
As one pastor said, "You can trust Jesus to get you there
because He already blazed
the path before you."

God IS!

God knows the worst about us,
the very worst, and still loves us.
We needn't worry about Him learning
of some dastardly deed or habit or secret
and then cutting us off. He already knows
everything and His love remains infinite.
God also knows the very best about us, thoughts,
words and deeds no other person knows about:
how we've worked at studying His Word,
what our true motives were when we were
accused of wrong, what little deeds of kindness
and goodness we've done around the house or
work place just because they're right.
He knows it all. His love is a complete love,
not naive, not taken in, not hoodwinked.
He loves us each, as they say,
"with His eyes open."

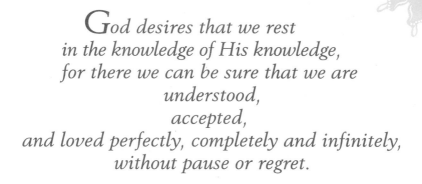

God desires that we rest
in the knowledge of His knowledge,
for there we can be sure that we are
understood,
accepted,
and loved perfectly, completely and infinitely,
without pause or regret.

God IS!

Did God know Satan would rebel?
That Adam and Eve would disobey?
Of course. Then why did He create them?
For the same reasons
any creator or artist does anything:
to test the limits and achieve something which,
in the end, will be stupendous.
Only a truly patient God
could put up with a man who calls Him
"Fool" to His face,
and then challenges Him to strike him dead
with lightning if he is not correct.

God is Wise!

*The wisdom of this world
is foolishness in God's sight.
As it is written:
"He catches the wise in their craftiness";
and again,
"The Lord knows that the thoughts
of the wise are futile."*

—1 Corinthians 3:19-20 NIV

God Is!

I firmly believe in Divine Providence.
Without belief in Providence
I think I should go crazy.
Without God the world would
be a maze without a clue.

—*Woodrow Wilson*

God Is!

A retired missionary was
to examine a missions candidate
one wintry morning.
The candidate arrived at 5 a.m. at the
examiner's home as planned,
but after being rushed into an office,
he sat waiting for three hours.
When the examiner finally arrived,
he didn't apologize but started his
examination with the question,
"Can you spell?"
"Yes, sir," the young man answered.
"Then spell 'baker'."
"B-A-K-E-R," the young man spelled,
clearly amazed but willing.
"Fine. Now, do you know
anything about numbers?"
"Yes, sir, a bit."

God Is!

"How much is two plus two?"
"Four," the candidate said calmly,
obviously mystified but not angry.
"Fine," said the examiner.
"You have passed.
I'll tell the board tomorrow."
At the board meeting,
the examiner gave this report:
"He has all the qualifications of a missionary.
First I tested him on self-denial,
making him arrive at 5 a.m.
He did so without complaining.
Second, I tested him on punctuality.
He arrived on time.
Third, I examined him on patience.
I made him wait three hours to see me.
Fourth, I tested him on temper.
He showed no anger the whole interview.
Fifth, I tried his humility by asking

God Is!

him questions that a seven-year old
could answer.
He showed no indignation.
He meets all the requirements."
Like that examiner,
God in His matchless wisdom rarely
works things out the way we'd expect,
but after all, what did we expect — He is God:
mysterious, inscrutable, awesome,
infinitely wise and loving
through to the heart.

God Is!

I *never saw a moor,*
I never saw the sea;
Yet know I how the heather looks,
And what a wave must be.
I never spoke with God,
Nor visited in heaven;
Yet certain am I of the spot
As if the chart were given.

—Emily Dickinson

God Is!

God in His wisdom knows
precisely when and where to inject
a little humor into a tense situation.
After the doctor had examined my wife,
who was going through a difficult pregnancy,
he turned to my then five-year old
daughter, Nicole, and asked,
"So you're going to have a little sister or brother?"
"Yup," Nicole answered,
quite absorbed in playing with her Barbie doll.
"And I guess you'll have to get the baby
at the supermarket?"
Nicole suddenly looked up,
disdain crinkling her features,
her Barbie halted in mid air.
"You know that's not where you
get babies, Dr. Modlin."
"Then where do you get them?" the doctor continued,

God Is!

winking at my wife.
Nicole pursed her lips,
then spoke precisely and
emphatically:
"From the baby doctor, of course!"

God Is!

"Proofs of God's wisdom?" some ask.
"None exist!"
Clarence Darrow said,
"In spite of all the yearnings of men,
no one can produce a single fact or
reason to support the belief in God and
in personal immortality."
Darrow, a lawyer, should have seen his folly.
For the proofs are all around us.
Look down, look up, look around and
you'll see God's handiwork.
Do you think stars and suns and trees and
birds came about by accident?
Look into your own heart and what do you see?
Lust, anger, greed, hatred, but also a longing to be
guided, to be understood, to be loved.
That's God talking in your heart.
That's God talking in creation through the apple,

God Is!

the blueberry, the panda, the penguin.
All of them point to Him, saying,
"This is what I have done.
Now what are you going to do with it?"
Claiming there are no "proofs" or facts
is preposterous. Millions exist.
Some people just refuse to look.

God Is!

Every Christian wonders at times
what's ahead in my life?
Where am I going?
Unfortunately, life isn't predictable.
For the Christian, whose life is ordered by
a God who often throws us the impossible once
a month or so, it can be a real rollercoaster.
Wouldn't it be nice if we could hand God
a list of things we don't want to happen in our lives?
"Lord, I can deal with anything but . . .
a handicapped child
AIDs
a wayward son or daughter
having to become a missionary
poverty
being fat
being single for the rest of my life
ending up a colossal failure . . . ."

God Is!

No, God hasn't offered us that
kind of deal.
Instead, He says to each of us,
"Trust Me. I know where I'm going,
I know what's best for you.
Let me plan your future and
I won't doublecross you."
Trusting God means believing that
He has the brains and the power
to get us to a destination
we wouldn't have missed for all the health,
wealth and prosperity this world can offer.

———◆———

God Is!

*Abraham Lincoln, perhaps one of the
wisest statesman who has ever lived, wrote,
"I should be the most presumptuous blockhead
upon this footstool if I for one day thought that
I could discharge the duties which have come upon me
since I came to this place, without the aid and
enlightenment of One who is stronger and
wiser than all others."
Oh for a legion of men and women
in political power
who had that outlook!*

God Is!

*Some people suppose that the Bible
is little more than a compendium of
commandments, all designed to strip from
us any pleasures we might have in life.
In reality, those commandments were spoken
to protect us from harm, to give us joy in the
doing and to fulfill us as His children.
My daughter was struggling with
understanding some science problems.
When I have helped her in the past,
she has become impatient and angry,
accusing me of thinking she's stupid.
This aggravated me to no end, but as I sat down to
work with her, it seemed God spoke in my heart,
"Just be patient. You were a kid once, too.
She desperately wants your respect and love.
So give it to her. Remember, 'a gentle answer turns
away wrath, but a harsh word stirs up anger'."*

God Is!

*I spoke softly and worked with Nicole
through the problems. We had
several fits and false starts, but in time she
got it. At the end, she said, "Thanks, Daddy.
Now I really do understand it."
I kissed her and told her I loved her.
Later I overheard her say to my wife,
"It went really good this time.
He didn't get mad at me or anything."
God's commands are never
burdensome to those who will obey.
They're His way of saying,
"Follow Me in this matter and
I will lead you into an adventure
you would not have missed
for all the tea in China,
all the gold in Ft. Knox
or all the nickels in Nickelodeon."*

God Is!

*Sometimes Christians get the idea
that God is only in this project called
redemption for His own pleasure and
fulfillment. He'll use us for His glory, then
dispose of us regardless of any dreams and hopes
we may have built up along the way.
Like the football rookie I read about who longed to
get into a game.
Finally, in the middle of a tough contest
the coach called him.
The lad whipped off his warm-up coat and ran over,
fully expecting to be sent in to make a last
second grab for a touchdown.
Nothing of the sort. The coach told him,
"We've run out of time-outs!
Go in there and get hurt!"
Some folks imagine that God uses His people like
that rookie — with no concern for their*

God Is!

feelings or desires.
But that is never true of the God
who is both infinitely wise and
impeachably loving.
God's plan is not only that He be praised
and worshiped and loved, but that we be
fulfilled, satisfied and completed as
His people at the same time.
He came "that we might have life,
and have it abundantly."

God Is!

Isaac Newton, the great mathematician and discoverer of the Law of Gravity, said, "In the absence of any other proof, the thumb alone would convince me of God's existence."

———•———

God Is!

Sometime ago my daughter
Nicole fell and a piece of metal
gouged out a hole in her shin.
When she staggered back to the house
in tears, I took one look and knew we had to
rush her to the emergency room. I could see the
glint of white bone at the bottom of the cut.
At the hospital, Nicole curled up in pain,
not wanting anyone to touch
the wound or go near it.
The doctor promised her he wouldn't hurt her,
but she moaned and pled,
covering the wound with her hand,
terrified he would inflict more torment.
Though I can sometimes endure much personal pain,
seeing my children in agony of any sort
is a heart-rending experience.
Tears burned my eyes as I watched,

God Is!

Nicole's agonized appeals piercing
me to the heart.
Finally, after fifteen minutes of
rebuffed assurances,
the doctor became impatient and told the
nurses to hold Nicole down.
He seized a needle and injected its
numbing liquid directly into the wound.
I watched in horror and Nicole screamed,
the emergency room reverberating
with her pained cries.
Not knowing what else to do,
I grabbed Nicole's hand and squeezed, saying,
"It'll be over in a second, honey.
Just hold on. Please just hold on."
Finished, the anesthesia numbed the wound and
after a few minutes of tears and sniffling,
Nicole settled down. I patted her hand,
greatly relieved she felt better, and said,

God Is!

"I'm sorry it hurt so much, honey."
She replied sheepishly,
"I'm sorry I screamed."
I smiled, that blood-curdling shriek still
echoing in my mind. I said,
"That's okay. sometimes we need to scream."
"I know," she said. "And if you hadn't
held my hand, I would've screamed worse."
I laughed, but it made me think of a
truth I often forget:
God in His wisdom does let us hurt.
But He always comforts us, sending someone to
hold our hand or cool our brow or weep with us,
knowing that without them we
"would have screamed worse."

God Is!

*I worried for a long time as a
new Christian that God might
"call" me overseas to become a missionary.
And not just any missionary. No, I was
convinced God would send me to a country
where I'd live in a mud hut infested with snakes
and cockroaches, where I'd wear little more
than a breechcloth, and where my food —
when I could get some — would consist mostly
of roots I'd have to dig in the nearby jungle.
I kept picturing this scene where the cannibals
I came to convert were dancing around my hut,
yelling and screaming in maniacal glee
because they were going to eat me that night.
I'd see myself stepping out to preach the gospel
and immediately, they'd hurl spears
and fire arrows into my body.
I'd fall down dead, a martyr for the faith.*

God Is!

*At that point, I'd smugly imagine all
the pastors in the U.S. telling my story
and encouraging the faithful to be as
"committed" as me. Despite the imagined praise,
though, I was terrified God would actually send me
to this place. I finally talked to a pastor about it,
and he asked me, Well, if God decides you don't have
to be a missionary to this roach-infested,
cannibalistic place, what would you do instead?"
"I'd be a minister and write books and novels for
Christians to encourage them," I said. The pastor replied,
"Well, why doesn't God want you to do that now?"
"I guess because that would be fun!"
He shook his head.
"It's amazing how many Christians think God wants
them to do something they'd consider awful.
It's also amazing how many think
God's against fun."*

God Is!

Today I have to agree:
Why do we think God would
never want us to do something we'd
consider fulfilling, exciting, even fun?
I guess it all goes back to our fallen nature.
In truth, God is not only pleased to see us
having a ball working out "His will for our lives,"
but He has also promised to throw in joy,
peace, love and everything else to make it
even more satisfying.

God Is!

One of the most remarkable stories
I have ever heard about Abraham Lincoln
happened in his younger years.
He and his partner, Berry, owned a little
country store that stood on the verge of ruin.
When both men realized their business had failed,
Lincoln said, "You know I wouldn't mind so
much if I could just do what I want to do.
I want to study law. If we could only sell
everything we've got and pay all our bills and
have just enough left over to buy one book,
Blackstone's commentary on English law,
I would not mind it at all, but I guess we can't."
At that point, a wagon rattled up the road.
When the driver spotted Lincoln and Berry,
he asked if they might buy a barrel
he had for fifty cents. He was out of money,
but had a long journey ahead to reach the west where

God Is!

he and his young wife were headed.
Lincoln peered into the eyes of the
poor, thin woman on the wagon seat and,
being a man of great compassion,
he reached into his pocket,
pulling out his last fifty cents.
"I reckon I could use a good barrel," he said.
The barrel sat on the porch all that day,
with Berry laughing about his partner's
foolishness, but late in the evening Lincoln noticed
some papers lying down in the bottom of it.
He reached in and his hand grasped a book.
Lifting it out, he read the title on the cover and
stood petrified: it was Blackstone's commentary.
Lincoln later said,
"I stood there holding the book,
looking up toward the heavens. There came a
deep impression on me that God
had something for me to do and He was

God Is!

*showing me now that
I had to get ready for it.
Why this miracle otherwise?"
Some might call this an incredible
coincidence. The Christian, though, sees it the
same way Lincoln did:
as the finger of the only wise God.*

God Is!

*Sometimes we get the impression
from the media that most scientists
are atheists or agnostics.
On the contrary, I have rarely met
a man of science who wasn't a believer
on some level. A biologist told me,
"The more I study the way things are put together,
the more I'm convinced it was done by a wise
Creator and not a chancy,
impersonal process like evolution.
In fact, I find it easier to believe in a Creator
over evolution for the very reason that
it's easier to believe my wife's GE microwave
oven was designed and fashioned by
intelligent engineers than because someone
threw a box of parts into my kitchen,
set them afire and out came this oven!"
Study creation long enough and you can't help*

God Is!

but marvel over what God has done.
And if God can create something as
complex and perfect and beautiful as the
human body, isn't it probable
He can also make your life beautiful, too?

The foolishness of God
is wiser than man's wisdom,
and the weakness of God
is stronger than man's strength.

—1 Corinthians 1:25, *NIV*

"For My thoughts are not your thoughts,
Neither are your ways My ways,"
declares the LORD.
"For as the heavens are higher than the earth,
So are My ways higher than your ways,
And My thoughts than your thoughts."

—*Isaiah 55:8-9* NASB

God is Good!

*Give thanks to the LORD, for He is good;
For His lovingkindness is everlasting.*

—Psalm 136:1 NASB

God Is!

*When Josef Stalin's daughter
defected from Communist Russia,
her story startled millions. How could she,
the daughter of one of the most powerful men
on earth, leave home and refuge and
all the privileges of her family's position?
Her words to the press told the story:
"I found it was impossible to exist without God
in one's heart. I came to that conclusion myself,
without anybody's help or preaching.
That was a great change because since that
moment, the main dogmas of Communism
lost their significance to me. I have come here
to seek the self-expression that has been
denied me so long in Russia."
When God opens a heart, He frees a soul.*

God Is!

A relationship with God ebbs and flows, rises and falls upon the emotions and needs of each believer.

It is never static. At times, our ardor and zeal fade and we sometimes yearn to return to the "glory days" when God's power and goodness surged through us like a geyser.

In a London church lies a bronze tablet that says, "Here God laid his hands on William Booth." Booth was the founder of the Salvation Army and a multitude of works helping orphans, the poor and the needy.

One day a man stopped at the church and stood near the tablet for several hours, staring at it.

Finally, it came time to close and the caretaker asked him to leave. "Just one minute more," the visitor begged. The caretaker was waiting in the shadows when he

God Is!

heard the man pray fervently,
"O God, do it again!"
He was William Booth.
I felt compassion for that great Christian
when I read that. Perhaps Booth was
depressed, or had suffered setbacks,
or maybe he'd just had a bad day.
But I suspect God had just as firm a hold of him
then as He did that first time in the church.
God doesn't ever let us go;
He simply employs us in His work in
different ways at different times.

God Is!

How *great is Thy goodness,*
Which Thou hast stored up for those who fear
Thee, Which Thou hast wrought
for those who take refuge in Thee,
Before the sons of men! O love the LORD,
all you His godly ones!
The LORD preserves the faithful,
And fully recompenses the proud does.
Be strong, and let your heart take courage,
All you who hope in the LORD.

—Psalm 31:19, 23-24 NASB

God Is!

God don't make no mistakes
— that's how He got to be God.
—Archie Bunker on the 60's show, All In the Family
No, Archie. Yes, God doesn't make mistakes,
but God didn't get to be God.
He doesn't make mistakes because
He is God,
always was,
and always will be.

God Is!

God gave us memory
so that we might have roses
in December.

—Sir J. M. Barrie

God Is!

It's interesting that in war, both sides often proclaim God is on their side. They even pray that He will let them win. Hitler himself said, "Who says I am not under the special protection of God?" And don't forget the words of John Wayne in the movie, The Longest Day: "Sometimes I wonder whose side God's on!" Likewise, people who attain great success frequently thank God for helping them win the prize, even though many others probably prayed the same prayer but didn't get the same answer. How does God work this out? How does He decide who wins and who loses, who succeeds and who fails? How does God choose when two deserving believers pray for the same award but only one can win?

God Is!

*Undoubtedly, God has sane and
intelligent reasons for all His choices,
but He has not revealed
His reasons for them now.
Maybe Billy Graham said it best.
When people ask him why God has
so exalted him in our times, he answers,
"I'm going to be the first one to ask
Him that when I get to heaven."*

*To be good is noble;
but to show others how to be good
is nobler and no trouble.*

—Mark Twain

"God is so good,
God is so good,
God is so good,
He's so good to me . . ."

—Contemporary song lyric

God Is!

On occasion I wonder how God
looks at us, what He feels when He sees
us in the midst of some job or project.
Pride? Joy? Compassion? Love?
One day we bought my daughter Nicole,
then four years old, a pair of new shoes.
She could talk of nothing else and when I put her to bed,
she wanted to wear the shoes as she slept.
I told her, "No, we don't wear shoes to bed."
Later, I walked upstairs to go to bed myself and
looked in on her. She lay asleep, clutching her
stuffed dog. There, on the dog's front feet,
were her shoes, neatly tied and tight.
I smiled, and suddenly a voice spoke in my heart,
"How did you feel when you saw your daughter like
that, Mark?" I laughed. "I don't know.
Love. Pride. Joy. The usual things."
The voice whispered, "That's how I feel, only bigger."

God Is!

*Luis Bunuel once wrote,
"Thanks be to God, I am still an atheist."
His joke contains a powerful truth:
Why does God let atheists live,
not only to corrupt their own lives,
but also the lives of others?
I asked this in a class and someone answered,
"For one reason: because if He started slaying
people the moment they stopped
believing or started disbelieving,
He'd probably have to kill off most Christians
several times a day."*

God Is!

Praise the LORD!
Oh give thanks to the LORD,
for He is good;
For His lovingkindness is everlasting.

—Psalm 106:1 NASB

God Is!

*Some say God had to let evil invade His
universe so that He could show Himself off.
After all, against the inky black backdrop
of our sinful world His snow-white character
shines rather brightly.
The idea, though, is a mistake.
If God let evil erupt into this world with all
the carnage and agony that has resulted just to
make Himself look good,
He wouldn't look good or be good at all;
He'd look like a monstrous manipulator,
worse than Hitler, Stalin and Mao combined.*

God Is!

Sometimes people say they do not
believe in God because they have never
seen proof of His existence.
A fanciful story about some mice living
in a piano illustrates this.
All around them, wonderful music resounded and
the mice came to believe that a Great Unseen
Player made the music. It comforted them to
think that this Someone cared about them
enough to fill their lives with beautiful
sonatas, anthems and songs.
One day, though, a mouse climbed up higher in the
piano and found the wires that made the sounds.
He told all the other mice and soon they all
knew the secret: the wires made the music,
not a Great Unseen Player.
In time, another mouse trekked skyward and
found the hammers that hit the wires.

God Is!

Again, the mice revised their beliefs:
they really did live in a perfectly
mechanical world for which
everything had a natural explanation.
The mice ridiculed the idea of the
Great Unseen Player and few thanked
Him anymore for the music.
In our world, we find "mechanical"
explanations for circumstances and events,
and this, some believe, rules out God,
the Great Unseen Player who orchestrates.
Nonetheless, that doesn't mean He isn't
the One doing it.
Or that He will stop playing.

*L*ife is hard
by the yard.
But by the inch
life is a cinch.

—Jean L. Gordon

God Is!

God gave us the universe to be our playground,
and He has stocked it with so many pleasures
and wonders that we need never become bored
or jaded. Unbelief makes us give in to such
attitudes, and even then it's remarkable how
an agnostic or atheist can partake of a
McCown apple or a slice of
"Decadent Chocolate Cheesecake"
or some such delectable and still proclaim,
"If there is a God, He must be a beast."

God Is!

*As for you, you meant evil against me,
but God meant it for good
in order to bring about this present result,
to preserve many people alive.*

*—Joseph to his brothers,
about them selling him into slavery.
Genesis 50:20 NASB*

God Is!

Going to church doesn't make you a Christian any more than going to a garage makes you a car.

—Laurence J. Peter

But going to church might help.
In fact, if it is the right kind of church,
it should help.

God is All-Powerful!

*And I heard, as it were,
the voice of a great multitude and
as the sound of many waters and
as the sound of mighty peals of thunder,
saying, "Hallelujah! For the Lord our God,
the Almighty, reigns."*

—*Revelation* 19:6 NASB

God Is!

*Jesus says in John, "If any man is thirsty,
let him come to Me and drink."
The main mistake we make is coming
to Him with a thimble when
He would rather we brought a bucket.
Or a hundred buckets.*

———◆———

God Is!

*Lord Acton gave us the famed quote,
"Power tends to corrupt;
absolute power corrupts absolutely."
This is true in the case of men,
especially politicians, kings and presidents.
But with God, who does possess absolute power,
there is no corruption.
Why? Because His power is wedded
to absolute goodness, absolute holiness and
absolute love.
The reason power corrupts men is
because men are by nature corrupt,
not because power itself is.*

God Is!

*Evangelist Grady Wilson spoke
of an old fellow named Uncle Buddy Robinson.
The man didn't feel up to par one week and
visited the doctor. After an examination
the doctor informed him he had diabetes.
"What's that?" Uncle Buddy asked.
"You have too much sugar in your blood,"
the doctor told him.
For a second, Uncle Buddy looked amazed.
Then he whooped. "Well, praise the Lord.
I been praying that God'd make me a
sweet old man and he overdone it."*

God Is!

One of Woody Allen's
jokes goes like this:
"If it turns out that there is a God,
I don't think that he's evil.
But the worst that you can say about him is
that basically he's an underachiever."
Many people accept this idea,
even if it's not stated quite so boldly.
Why? Because, they reason,
if God were really all-powerful,
good, loving and wise,
He'd have fixed the problem of evil by now.
Surely, murder, genocide, hatred, prejudice,
robbery, abuse, etc. would have been scoured
away from humanity by the twentieth century —
if God were good, loving, etc. etc.
But think about it:
if God decided to wipe out all evil today,

God Is!

...would any of us even exist tomorrow?
God is dealing with evil now and has
been since the beginning of human history.
He promises one day He will banish it
from His creation forever,
never to rise again.
Until then, all we can do is watch and wait,
and allow Him to use us to deal with
the evil in our own hearts.

When I pray, coincidences happen;
and when I don't, they don't.

—William Temple

God Is!

God is so powerful that He rarely
chooses to show off that power.
First of all, any true demonstration of His
infinite power would scare most of us to death.
Second, He doesn't need to show off anything;
He already knows what He can do and
doesn't require our oohs and aahs to make
Him feel powerful and important.
This is the principal difference between
God and the average politician.

God Is!

*F*or He spoke, and it was done;
He commanded, and it stood fast.
The LORD nullifies the counsel of the nations;
He frustrates the plans of the peoples.
The counsel of the LORD stands forever,
The plans of His heart from generation to generation.

—*Psalm 33:9-11* NASB

God Is!

Many ask,
"How can a loving and all-powerful God
allow suffering and evil?"
They think either God isn't all-powerful and
therefore can do nothing about evil,
or He isn't love and therefore doesn't care.
The Bible teaches He is both
all-powerful and perfectly loving.
He has chosen to let evil flourish for a short time,
perhaps to convince us what a monstrosity evil truly is.
In its right time,
He will deal with evil once and for all.
It will never again have power
or presence in His creation.
Until then,
He asks us to trust Him to get us there.

God Is!

God is all-powerful,
but in working with creatures like us
who have wills and spirits,
He must woo us into godly living not
by the cudgel but by the carrot.
He "motivates" us to want to live for Him
by not only showing us how to live right,
but by answering why we should obey Him.
He gave the Ten Commandments not as
ten policemen keeping us from the delicacies,
but as ten protectors helping us avoid the destroyers.
He tells us in them,
"Avoid these things because they will kill you."
Not, "Avoid these things or I will kill you!"
Ben Franklin once helped a chaplain
"encourage" soldiers at a frontier fort to
come to prayer meeting.
Franklin noticed that the men were allowed a

God Is!

small ration of rum each day,
so he told the chaplain to act not only
as "rum steward,"
but also to dispense the rum right after prayers.
The chaplain agreed and Franklin later
noted in his diary,
"Never were prayers more generally or
more punctually attended."
Though God doesn't recommend giving us gin
in return for prayer,
He does provide some carrots along the way,
like assuring us,
"I will answer speedily" and
"Ask, and you shall receive!"

God Is!

A Scottish preacher named
McLeod Campbell was once asked
by a friend struggling with doubt,
"Pastor, you always seem to have such
peace of soul. Tell me, how can you feel
that you've got such a tight hold on God?"
The pastor squinted with thought,
then beamed a smile and exclaimed,
"I don't always feel that I have hold of Him,
but praise the Lord,
I know that He always has hold of me!"

God Is!

*It's not always easy to trust God.
His way of doing things is not always
our way, as Isaiah wrote (55:8-9).
With that in mind, I have always liked
the story about the man who tumbled over
a cliff and was saved only by grabbing a bush
growing just under the edge.
He hung there for a moment, then cried out,
"Please, is there someone up there to help me?"
Suddenly, a majestic voice boomed above him,
"I am here!"
"Who are you?"
"God!"
"Oh, thank God!" the man cried.
"Please save me!"
"Do you trust Me?" God boomed.
"Yes! Of course."
"Then let go of the bush."*

God Is!

There was an embarrassing silence.
Then the man yelled,
"Is anyone else up there?"
That's me. That's you.
When we get hung out over the cliff,
we know our only hope is in God.
But then He wants us to do something crazy!
And yet, if He always made sense,
wouldn't we have thought of the way out of trouble
without Him?

If the work of God could be comprehended by
reason, it would be no longer wonderful.

—Gregory the Great

God Is!

*J*ewish novelist, Bernard Malamud,
told the story of a pious man who
hit hard times and prayed,
"Please let me win the Lottery, God.
It's only right in view of all the years
I've believed in You."
The next day the man waited, but nothing happened.
He prayed again that night,
but the next day he won nothing.
Finally, the third day,
he fell to his knees and complained,
"Why don't You give me a break, God?"
Suddenly the Almighty spoke,
his voice booming in the small chamber,
"Why don't you give Me a break?
At least buy a ticket!"
Even God's omnipotence is not great enough
to answer a prayer that has no "get up and go."

God Is!

Dr. Donald Grey Barnhouse spoke
at a church filled with students,
free thinkers and skeptics.
During the question and answer session that
followed, a young man stood and asked,
"How is it possible for millions of Jews to wander
years in the wilderness without their shoes wearing out,
without their clothes wearing out,
without going hungry and without going thirsty?"
With Bible in hand, Dr. Barnhouse gazed
out over the crowd, then quietly intoned,
"God!"
The youth replied, "Thank you, Dr. Barnhouse,
now I understand."
The sage preacher replied, "No, you don't, son.
No one understands."
How can God be all-powerful?
How could He create out of nothing?

God Is!

How could He part the Red Sea?
Or heal a leper instantaneously?
Or raise His Son from the dead?
No one knows.
He's God.
This is who He is.
We can accept it, reject it,
argue about it or complain it's impossible.
But maybe that's why we worship
Him and no other,
for He alone is worthy.

———◦●◦———

God Is!

*M*ortimer Adler,
editor of the Encyclopedia Britannica
and The Great Books,
taught classes on religion in his early years.
He spent much time leading his students
to understand of St. Thomas Aquinas' "proofs"
of the existence of God.
In most of his classes, the students succumbed
one by one to both Aquinas' and Adler's arguments.
But one young man named Charles Adams
refused to budge from his agnostic position.
As Adler and Adams locked mental horns,
they made no progress.
Then an assistant suggested that the professor
tell the class about Aquinas' life and work rather
than simply discuss his arguments.
Adler quickly reeled off the story of how Aquinas,
a monk living under austere conditions without

God Is!

a library, a typewriter or other help,
in twenty years produced several shelves'
worth of books that became the worldwide
standard of Christian theology.
Adler added that most of those works
contained numerous quotations from the Bible,
the early church fathers, the Greek and
Roman philosophers and many other writers
up to the 12th century.
In many cases Aquinas cited them by memory.
Somehow, Adler told them,
Aquinas accomplished all this without a well-stocked
library or a modern filing system.
As Adler discussed about this incredible
intellectual achievement,
Adams interrupted and rebuked him,
"Why didn't you tell us all this before?"
Adler asked, "Why?"

God Is!

The student answered,
"Because if you had told us
all this about Aquinas,
you would not have had to bother our
minds with arguments about
God's existence.
Aquinas could not have done
what he did without God's help."

"God is really only another artist.
He invented the giraffe, the elephant,
and the cat.
He has no real style.
He just goes on trying other things."

—*Pablo Picasso*

God Is!

*Sometimes the best way to move a person
toward faith in God is not to list
God's qualities and attributes as if
He were little more than that list,
but to tell them of God's work
in our lives — simply,
plainly and without embellishment.*

God Is!

*Grace and peace be multiplied to you in the
knowledge of God and of Jesus our Lord;
seeing that His divine power has granted
to us everything pertaining to life and godliness.*

—2 Peter 1:2-3 NASB

God is Everywhere!

Where can I go from Your Spirit?
Or where can I flee from Your presence?
If I ascend into heaven, You are there;
If I make my bed in hell, behold, You are there.
If I take the wings of the morning,
And dwell in the uttermost parts of the sea,
Even there Your hand shall lead me,
And Your right hand shall hold me.

—Psalm 139:7-10 NKJV

God Is!

I searched for God
on the highest mountain,
in the lowest valley,
in the deepest forest;
then I found him
in the rainbow-hued bubbles
on the water with which
I scrubbed my kitchen floor.

—Charlotte Carpenter

God Is!

*G*od's omnipresence wonderfully
brings God down to our level.
At the same time, it allows Him room
to be completely Himself.
An atheist wanted to show his neighbor,
a common laborer, how foolish his religion was.
Finding the laborer on the road on a Sunday morning,
the atheist asked, "Where are you going, sir?"
"To church, my friend," the laborer replied.
"What will you do there?"
"Worship God, as always."
The atheist smiled wickedly, sure a kill was at hand.
He said, "Is your God a great God, or a small God?"
The laborer laughed. "He is both, sir.
He is so great that the heavens cannot contain Him,
and He is so small,
that He can dwell in my poor heart."
Stumped and dismayed,

God Is!

the atheist departed, grumbling
about the foolishness of it all.
But that laborer went his way rejoicing.
For he was right: God is infinite,
too huge to fit into the confines of
the known universe.
Yet He is also small enough to sit by our beds
and refresh us when we are sick,
plain enough to speak out of
His Word and give us hope,
personal enough to lead us through a dark alley
when we can't go around.
God is, in a word,
enough for all of us and then some.

God Is!

All Christians struggle to comprehend
the great doctrines of scripture,
especially those about God's attributes.
"How can God be three persons
and yet one?" some ask.
Or, "How can God be everywhere at once when
He is One?"
Or,
"How can God hear the prayers of millions
every day, and never get confused,
never lose an answer?"
No one can explain it.
But that doesn't mean it's true.
If we could completely understand God,
we would be greater than God and
wouldn't need Him!
Mrs. Albert Einstein once illustrated this idea
when someone asked her if she understood her

God Is!

*husband's Theory of Relativity.
She laughed and replied,
"No, I don't understand it at all.
But I do understand Professor Einstein,
and that's all that really matters."
While we may not comprehend all the exhausting
theology about God, we can easily understand
that He is here, with me, now; that He listens
to all I say and ask and think; that He knows
me through to my most secret thoughts;
and that He loves me enough to die for me.
These are profound truths, with tremendous
theology behind them, yet they're simple enough
for a child to hold sure and dear.
As one boy said when kids ridiculed his
faith on the playground, "Jesus is my friend.
He goes with me wherever I go.
He's right here and He knows all about what's
happening here.*

God Is!

*And He keeps telling me,
'Don't worry about those kids.
They're just full of hot air!' So there!"
Maybe that boy should have quoted
Psalm 14:1 to them:
"The fool has said in his heart,
there is no God."*

"God has tried again and again to speak to me,
but I wouldn't listen."

—Oliver Wendell Holmes

God Is!

*Sometimes people take the truth of
God's omnipresence a little too far.
In one case, a mother asked her young
son to grab a broom from the back porch.
Late in the evening, the boy hesitated
because it looked dark and scary out there.
He said, "Mommy,
didn't you say God was everywhere?"
"Of course," replied the mother.
The boy pulled open the porch door,
leaned out and called,
"God, would you please hand me the broom?"
If only He would, how much simpler would my day
go when I am fixing up things around the house!
As one pastor said,
"God is not a go-fer; He's a 'good-fer;'
good fer salvation; good fer hope;
good fer comfort on a dark, rainy night."*

God Is!

*The Psalm says if you go
up into heaven, God is there.
If you go down into the pit,
He's there, too. No, not just there.
He, in His whole being, is at each spot,
for each person, at every moment of history.
That means when you pray,
you have God's complete and undivided attention.
When you have a need, He's fully there,
doing what's required to help.
When you need advice, you never get a busy signal.
He's there on the sofa with you.
Or in the shop. Or on the track.
We cannot flee from Him; He goes with us.
We cannot hide from Him; He sees and knows
what we feel before we've even expressed it.
Omnipresent. The big word is "ubiquitous."
The little word is "here and now." Always and ever.*

God Is!

*Robert Owen, the Welsh reformer
and founder of the New Harmony,
Indiana utopian community,
often visited the coal mines of England.
On one trip, he spoke with a twelve-year old boy,
covered with coal-dust and worn out from
fourteen hours on the slag heaps. He asked the lad,
"Do you know God?" The boy replied,
"No. He must work in some other mine."
Such experiences can shred our belief
in a good God. Why? we ask.
Why does God do nothing?
But has God done nothing?
No, he stirred up reformers like
Owen to make child labor illegal.
He raised up men like George Muller
to provide homes and friendship for such boys.
And He called others to open their homes and*

God Is!

pray and offer help to orphans in need.
Sure, God didn't wipe the evil of
child labor out in an hour.
In fact, I have read that in
some places like India it still exists.
But He has set Himself against it and
He works through His people to change the law,
change the system and change hearts.
The person of faith trusts that one day evil will be gone,
ended forever. But until that day we work,
with Him in our hearts and His tools in our hands,
to push back the tide that might otherwise
take us all away.

---

*Jesus answered and said to him,
"If anyone loves Me, he will keep My word;
and My Father will love him,
and We will come to him,
and make Our abode with him."*

—*John 14:23* NASB

God Is!

One of my preacher friends,
a liberal who espouses views I wouldn't
expect of a tomcat, waxed eloquent on God's
omnipresence one afternoon, saying it was
illogical to imagine someone being in two places at
one time. When he finished, I couldn't resist saying,
David, you've convinced me it is possible for
someone to be in two places at once.
You've just proven to me that
you can be talking to me here
and out to lunch at the same time."

God Is!

How is it possible for God to be in two or more places at once? It's actually fairly simple. Physically, it is impossible. But God is not physical; He's spirit. He is also not confined by time, because He's eternal. A Person who is both spirit and eternal sees human history like a completed video. He can view and spiritually "jump into" the video at any moment, then switch to another time and place, before or after, without disturbing the basic nature of the video. He can endlessly "tinker" with it, without losing any time whatsoever, because He is not "in" time, He is beyond it. Ultimately, for God, human history is a "done deal." He steps into it where He likes, when He likes and as often as He likes, without ever running out of time or energy.

Wherever we are, God is.
God is, wherever we are.
That can be scary, or intensely reassuring,
depending on what you
happen to be doing at the time.

God Is!

Children sometimes offer
a sobering look at this truth about
God's omnipresence that adults might miss.
For instance, a friend was helping her three-year
old daughter get ready for bed.
As Mom pulled off the day's dirty clothing,
the little girl suddenly asked,
"Is God here, Mommy?"
Mom, glad her daughter seemed to be awakening
to a great new spiritual truth,
replied enthusiastically,
"Yes, of course He is, honey."
The little girl burst the bubble when she replied,
"Well, would you ask Him to go out while
I'm undressing?"

When we have nothing else to lean on,
not even ourselves, He is still there."

—Philip Yancey

God Is!

When I left the ministry in 1984,
I went to work for my father.
I worried at the time,
never having worked for Dad as a employee
and I wondered how it would turn out.
For nine years I worked at his company.
I found it an amazing experience.
I could walk anytime I wanted into his office
and talk about whatever was on my mind.
As I watched him lead staff meetings,
my opinion of him enlarged for I witnessed
to his cool head, his calm gentility
and his plain-speaking integrity.
I went on trips and met other men
who had worked with him, and frequently
they volunteered the most uplifting compliments,
like the man who told me, "Your father is probably
the best salesman in our industry. Utterly honest."

God Is!

*At the end of my time with Dad's
company, the staff always threw a
special pizza party where the departing
employee gave a speech.
I thought long and hard about what I might
say. Finally, I settled on these words:
"When I was a kid,
I thought of my dad as Mr. Fix-it.
He could fix anything, and I brought him plenty
of toys and bikes that he usually set right.
When I got to college, I thought of Dad as my banker.
He provided the bread while I loafed.
When I went into the ministry,
Dad became my adviser, often helping me through
difficult situations that would have left many others
confused and bitter.
But when I came to this company,
I found something else in him I never could have
predicted: my dad became my friend."*

God Is!

*The room had been dead quiet
the whole time and I didn't know
how it had been received until
Dad told me afterwards,
"You almost had us all bawling there,
Mark. But everyone was very impressed,
most notably myself. Thanks for your words.
I feel the same way."
Sometimes I think my own journey with Jesus
has been like my relationship with my dad:
first, Mr. Fix-it.
Second, banker.
Next, advisor. Finally, friend.
I wonder what's next.*

God is Holy!

*In the year of King Uzziah's death,
I saw the Lord sitting on a throne,
lofty and exalted, with the train of
His robe filling the temple.
Seraphim stood above Him, each having six wings . . .
And one called out to another and said,
"Holy, Holy, Holy, is the LORD of hosts,
The whole earth is full of His glory."*

—Isaiah 6:1-3 NASB

God IS!

Holiness is very nearly the most
mysterious thing we know about God.
It's the only characteristic repeated
three times in the Bible in a
single sentence: "Holy, holy, holy . . ."
It's God's ultimate defining characteristic.
He is holy.
Unreachable.
Unimpeachable.
Unbreachable.
Utterly apart.
Utterly above and beyond all of us.
No one can touch Him for goodness,
righteousness, justice, grace.
No one can equal Him in power,
knowledge or presence.
Holiness, though, puts Him beyond all these
into a place we can hardly conceive of,

God IS!

a height infinitely beyond anything
we could be or dream of being.
Holiness makes Him worthy of respect,
reverence, love, worship.
Holiness seals all
His other attributes.
Because He is holy,
we can know He will never betray us,
never give up on us, never cease to love us.
Because He is holy,
we can trust Him for and with everything.

David Livingstone once asked an African chief what holiness was.
The chief replied,
"When showers have fallen in the night and the earth is washed clean, and when the sun sparkles on every leaf and the air is fresh — that is holiness."

God IS!

*While employed as personal secretary
to President Theodore Roosevelt,
Messmore Kendall found that
no matter how perfectly he typed a letter,
the President always made a correction or
scrawled a postscript.
Finally, Kendall asked T.R.,
"Are these mistakes mine,
or do you just change your mind about the
wording of every letter you dictate?"
"Neither," Roosevelt assured him.
"It's just that I've discovered people treasure
a letter from the President more when he has
added something in his own handwriting."
This made me think of the "personal touch" God
has brought to all His dealings with His people.
All through the Bible we see the personality of
God calling and lamenting and whispering in the*

God IS!

great stories of the faith.
Even as a new Christian,
I could feel the intimacy
He brought to the relationship.
When I prayed, there was an uncanny feeling
that He was sitting right there before me crosslegged
on the grass, nodding and listening intently.
When I read the Bible,
the words seemed uttered directly to me.
It sounds "mystical," but it is the
hallmark of God's down-to-earth personality:
He is real;
He is near;
He is holy;
He is a Person.

God IS!

*The Westminster Catechism tells us
that the chief end of man is to "love God
and enjoy Him forever."
The love part we get. But "enjoy" Him?
So many of us don't think of God as Someone to enjoy.
Worship? Yes. Obey? Certainly. But enjoy?
Recently my new wife Jeanette began introducing
many new pastimes into our family,
including playing games. "Sorry, Dutch Blitz,
Uno, Monopoly Junior,"
and others became events to look forward to.
One night, engaged in a deadly contest, all of us
shouting and laughing, my daughter Alisha, age
seven, exclaimed, "Daddy, I didn't know you knew
how to have fun!" I laughed, but it reminded me
of this truth. Not only is God good. Not only is
He holy and just and all-powerful and kind.
But sometimes He is even fun!*

one hundred fifty-three

God IS!

God is majestic
God is glorious.
God is unique.
God is utterly beyond and
above everything in His creation.
No one, no matter how pure, how good,
how righteous comes close to His perfectness,
His awesomeness.
These are all our feeble ways of saying
God is holy.

God IS!

*Too many times politicians have the
mistaken idea that goodness and
lawfulness can be legislated.
"Just pass some new laws," they say,
"and it will fix the problem."
In one story, some politicals complained bitterly that
the U.S. was just about the worst place
on the face of the earth.
A grim-faced man suddenly rose and said,
"What you seem to want, my friends,
is a place where every one must be good by law."
"That's it," the reformers agreed.
"Where smoking is not allowed and
such a thing as drink is unknown.
Where no one need worry about food and clothing. Where
everyone has to avoid hurting everyone else, and where
each keeps regular hours."
"Oh, to find such a place!"*

God IS!

one particularly soulful politician
oozed. "Easily found," said the man.
"I've just come out from doing
twelve years in one."
Neither laws nor cudgels will
make people get into line.
God Himself tried that with the
Law of Moses and look at the resulting disasters.
No, only one thing will bring in utopia,
and that is when the holy God Himself
sits on the throne of every human heart.

God IS!

Many years ago I remember
Muhammed Ali declaring to the world,
"I am the Greatest."
When it came to heavy-weight boxing,
indeed he was then numero uno.
But human greatness is relative.
When someone says he is the greatest,
we instinctively ask,
"Relative to who? To what?" We want to know:
Who exactly are you comparing yourself with?
A boy might declare to the ants in an anthill that
he is the greatest, the strongest, the most powerful.
But ultimately it doesn't mean much
(except perhaps to the ants).
When we speak of God's holiness,
we are saying He is the greatest.
Compared to what, to who?
To everyone and everything else in every way you

God IS!

*could catalogue it, except in
terms of sin and evil.
He is number one in a universe
where there is no number two,
no number three,
no number anything else.
Why? Because His brand of greatness is
so far beyond all others that the distance
between them is infinite, rendering
real comparison impossible.*

God IS!

True holiness of character means
being transformed into the image of
Christ. To be like Jesus is to be holy.
I think of the story of the poverty-stricken
crippled boy who was waiting for the subway in
New York City. When the train's doors opened,
the crowd rushed by so viciously that the boy was
knocked down, his legs trampled and
his crutches kicked yards away.
No one seemed to notice until a businessman quietly
picked up the boy's crutches,
helped the lad to his feet and then held the subway
doors as the boy stepped aboard.
Safe, the lad looked up into the man's friendly face
and asked, "Sir, could you tell me — are you Jesus?"
Our world is a dark place, and getting darker all the time.
Those who shine with the light of Christ will become
fewer and fewer. But God says those who will feed

God IS!

the hungry, give water to the thirsty, provide housing for the stranger, clothe the naked and visit the imprisoned are truly His.

———◦———

G*od is so completely the opposite of evil that, only when we see evil in action can we truly see God.*

God Is!

*W*hen men and women see God in
His holiness, the world is changed.
One preacher proclaimed,
"Romanism trembled when Martin Luther
saw God. The great awakening sprang into
being when Jonathan Edwards saw God.
The world became the parish of one man when
John Wesley saw God. Multitudes were saved when
George Whitefield saw God.
Thousands of orphans were fed when
George Mueller saw God." I might add,
"Racism was defeated when
Martin Luther King, Jr. saw God.
Lepers were comforted when Mother Teresa saw God.
And millions gained new hope when
Billy Graham saw God."
Only when we truly see God for who He is can we
become the kind of people the world sees as God's.

God IS!

*W*hen I attended church as a
teenager, one young woman in our
congregation was to me the epitome of
drabness and unattractiveness.
She always wore plain, dark clothing.
She never smiled.
She usually walked down the aisle right after
the choir, stiff and somber,
as if she were attending a funeral.
One day on the way home from church,
my parents and siblings discussed this girl,
and I asked what was wrong with her.
My dad replied, "'Well, I guess she's holy."
My seven-year old brother, well-known for his
insights from viewing too much television,
corrected Dad: "I don't think she's holy.
I think she has hemorrhoids."
I don't know whether my brother was right,

God IS!

but I know my dad was wrong. Only a faulty view of God can mistake a case of hemorrhoids for true holiness.

---

*All I have seen teaches me
to trust the Creator
for all I have not seen.*

—Ralph Waldo Emerson

God IS!

*When you meet someone who is
truly holy you probably won't think
of him or her as holy.
Rather, you'll see them as someone you
can trust, someone you could tell anything to
and know they will not share your confidences,
someone to whom you can delegate a job and
know that it will be done right, someone who will
give you an honest answer to any question.
Rarely do we think of holiness as holiness;
rather, we see it as beauty of spirit,
purity of soul, integrity of heart,
radiance of personality.
True holiness is so rare and so stunning and
provokes such a gut-level response,
that when we find it we're tempted either
to embrace it and make it our own,
or kill it and banish it from our sight forever.*

*The only way we know evil is evil is because
God is holy and holds everything in
His universe to His high standards.
Without a holy God,
evil wouldn't be evil;
it would be normal.*

God IS!

*Sometimes in prayer,
I'm tempted to treat God as
some lofty Potentate for whom only the
loftiest words are appropriate.
One of my professors used to call this
"scraping the Milky Way."
Though God is holy and august and
far greater than any of us, we need to be reminded
that we are also in His image,
and part of that image is the
playfulness we can sometimes bring to prayer.
It happened the day before Halloween when
my two daughters decided to color their hair pink
as part of their outfits.
I came upstairs to dinner and found two "pinkheads"
sitting at the table. "How do you like it?"
they both asked, laughing and chuckling.
"Beautiful," I said, not very sincerely.*

GOD IS!

I then said grace, intoning,
"Thank you, Lord, for this fine meal,
and thank you for the girls' hair."
This broke them up, of course,
until my wife said,
"Maybe we should thank Him that
they have hair at all."
I don't know what God thinks of such antics,
and I certainly don't want to make jokes of
something as important as prayer.
But I suspect God enjoys prayer most
when we can enjoy it, too.

Who is like You, O LORD, among the gods?
Who is like You, glorious in holiness,
Fearful in praises, doing wonders?

—Exodus 15:11 NKJV

God is Gracious!

*In your great mercy
you did not put an end to them or abandon them,
for you are a gracious and merciful God.*

—*Nehemiah 9:31* NIV

God Is!

On February 11, 1861,
Abraham Lincoln left his home
in Springfield, Illinois and began the
journey by train to Washington, DC,
where he would assume the office of
President of a nation divided by problems so
great that few thought he could succeed.
Lincoln, though, knew where to go for counsel.
When he stood on the rear platform of his
train car to speak to the people who had
gathered to see him off, he said,
"Today I leave you. I go to assume a task more
difficult than that which devolved upon
General Washington.
The great God which guided him must help me.
Without that assistance I shall surely fail;
with it, I cannot fail."
Many times over the next few years, Lincoln

God Is!

would fall to his knees, crying out to
God for guidance and wisdom.
He frequently turned to the Bible for help.
Some historians believe Lincoln was
converted to faith in Christ while in office.
Only God knows Abraham Lincoln's heart,
but his words ring loud and strong with a faith we
do not often see today in our leaders.
Why does God let us get ourselves into messes that
defy human wisdom and ability to resolve?
For only one reason:
so we will turn to Him who is grace
and wisdom itself, and there find
glad and lasting help.

God Is!

One day around Christmastime,
my daughter Nicole,
about seven years old,
found a Toys 'R Us catalogue and
began flipping through it.
I sat at the table perusing the paper as Nicole
showed me the pictures of the toys she wanted.
"I want this," she said about a Barbie doll.
"And I want this."
She pointed to a little Leggo house.
She stopped at a cuddly stuffed bear.
"I want this, too."
Soon she began flipping furiously through the
catalogue, stopping barely long enough to
breathe and say,
"I want this, and I want this, and I want this."
Then, as if knocked on the head, she stopped
and peered at me, her face lighting with

God Is!

a surge of insight.
"Daddy!" she exclaimed,
"I want everything!
Just buy me everything!"
I laughed, and thought of that verse in Ephesians:
"God has blessed us with every
spiritual blessing in the heavenly places."
How many blessings? Everyone of them!
God not only intends to give us far more than we can
wish for in the world to come, but far more than
we can even think of.

———◦•◦———

God Is!

*In C. S. Lewis' book,
"The Horse and His Boy,"
from the Narnia Chronicles,
a picture of God's protectiveness emerges as
the main character, Shasta, leaves all his friends
and treks on alone and hungry to carry
a message to the king.
On a dark and rainy road one night,
Shasta reviews his life, feeling everything
always goes wrong for him.
Suddenly, a Voice speaks out of the dark and Shasta
senses that some great creature walks beside him.
At first, he is afraid.
But he soon finds the Voice to be
benign and friendly.
The reader knows this Voice is Aslan,
the great lion who typifies Christ in the Chronicles,
but Shasta doesn't yet know Him.*

God Is!

As they talk, Shasta mentions what
bad luck it had been to meet
"so many lions" on his journey.
The Voice replies, "There was only one lion."
"What on earth do you mean?" Shasta cries.
"I've just told you there were at least
two the first night, and —"
"There was only one," the Voice answers,
"but he was swift of foot."
"How do you know?"
"I was the lion," the Voice says solemnly.
"I was the lion who forced you to join with Aravis.
I was the cat who comforted you among
the houses of the dead.
I was the lion who drove the jackals
from you while you slept.
I was the lion who gave the
Horses the new strength of fear for the last mile so
that you should reach King Lune in time.

God Is!

And I was the lion you do not
remember who pushed the boat in
which you lay, a child near death,
so that it came to shore where a man sat,
wakeful at midnight, to receive you."
"Then it was you who wounded Aravis?"
"It was I."
"What for?"
"Child," the Voice says,
"I am telling you your story, not hers.
I tell no one any story but his own."
"Who are you?" Shasta asks.
"Myself," says the Voice,
very deep and low so that the earth shook;
and again 'Myself,' loud and clear and gay;
and then the third time 'Myself,'
whispered so softly you could hardly hear it,
and yet it seemed to come from all round you
as if the leaves rustled with it.

God Is!

*That passage has always pictured for
me the wonderful ways God
protects and guides us.
He is never an uninvolved,
disinterested Lord and Master.
Always, He speaks to us in the dark
and woos us into the light, until,
our hearts brimming with love,
we embrace Him and entrust ourselves to Him,
without fear, without reserve, forever.*

God Is!

*W*hen God invites us to know Him,
He draws us into His light.
He encourages us to cease hiding,
to cease pretending, to end all the lies and
fabrications, to come as we are,
like the song says, "Just as I am."
The light tells us, even before we believe,
"Come. It's safe. I won't hurt you.
See, it's just a little doorway out of the darkness.
I promise, you won't be destroyed; in fact,
it'll be the greatest thing that will ever happen to you."
It's true. When we come to God into His light,
we need not fear being scorched or burned.
He is gentle, kind, never accusing, never belittling.
He shows us the truth only as we are able to
receive it. He leads in the way only as we
become ready to walk in it.
His light nudges us toward the truth with the lure

God Is!

of real food, real thirst-quenching
spiritual water, real life.
When we finally partake,
we are overwhelmed that the all-powerful,
all-knowing and infinitely holy God
is a creme-puff who at the drop of faith
is willing to give us everything — His kingdom,
His presence, His heart — and never look back.

—◆—

G*od has no problems,*
only plans.

—Corrie ten Boom

God Is!

God extends
His grace to every person.
He asks only that we believe
and follow His Son.
Faith is something anyone
can express
anywhere he or she is
anytime he or she desires.
God just can't make it any easier.

God Is!

*Hitler's armies had demolished
France and the Allies.
On May 26, 1940, tens of thousands of
British and French troops fled to the little
French town of Dunkirk on the Channel.
They were trapped.
No ships in the British Navy could rescue them,
being too large in the shallow waters.
The whole free world sat by their radios desperate,
terrified, praying for hope when there was no hope.
Then the miracle began. Early in the morning on
May 27, men and women set out,
the fishermen with their creaky leaky fishing craft,
the country gentlemen with their yachts,
the sportsmen with their racing motorboats.
They putt-putted across the Channel,
flaunting U-Boats and mines,
oblivious to the danger.*

God Is!

There they picked up ten, twenty,
thirty bedraggled soldiers and sped
them back to England. As they drove,
bullets pocked the water around them.
The German Luftwaffe raged overhead while
British Spitfires tried to hold off their fire.
Some boats sank. Others lost their crews,
or some of the soldiers. But the boats kept coming.
A hundred. A thousand.
All of them sleepless, dauntless, determined.
It continued for nine days.
338,226 men were saved.
It's perhaps the greatest war miracle of all time.
Winston Churchill later spoke over the airwaves,
"Let us therefore brace ourselves to our duties
and so bear ourselves that,
if the British Empire and the Commonwealth
last for a thousand years, men will say:
This was their finest hour." God's was the cross.

God Is!

*W*e talk about grace,
try to understand, but it escapes us.
We use expressions, like
"unmerited favor," "free gift," "divine charity."
Still, it's difficult.
But sometimes a picture helps.
Imagine a man, a thief. All his life a hustler,
first stealing pennies from his mother's wallet,
then lifting oranges at the local fruitstand.
Soon he's burglarizing homes, staging holdups
on the street, knocking over a bank or two.
He goes on like this for awhile.
Soon he's caught and sentenced. Death.
Stiff price, but he's dross. Scum.
Probably even his mother has written him off.
Of course, he's determined not to let them
humiliate him at the execution.
Stiff upper lip, he tells himself.

God Is!

No begging. Not even a prayer.
What did God ever do for him anyway?
They nail him up there with
one of his partners.
In the middle, there's someone else,
no one he's ever seen.
The crowd begins taunting him.
"Look at you now, thief!"
"Try and steal my wallet now, robber!"
"What you gonna do now, fool?"
He returns the abuse in spades.
"Come up here and fight like a man!"
"You're all gutless cowards!"
"I spit on you!"
Soon he can hardly breathe.
The pain in his arms magnifies.
He cries for some wine to deaden the pain.
But the Romans at the foot of his cross are gambling.
They don't even give him a glance.

God Is!

Then he notices something:
the crowd isn't yelling at him anymore;
they're screaming at the man
in the middle. Everyone,
even his partner on the third cross,
are shrieking. "Save yourself, prophet!"
"Where's God now, King?"
It's kind of fun, so he joins in despite his pain.
Then he remembers something about this one:
He's the Healer, the Nazarene,
the One some said was the Messiah.
He's not convinced, though.
"Yeah, save us, if You can, Nazarene!"
Even the crowd laughs at his joke.
The Nazarene on the middle says nothing, though,
except to forgive the Roman soldiers who
nailed Him in place, except to give His mother
over into the care of a friend,
except to look up into heaven and pray quietly,

God Is!

laboriously. At times their eyes meet,
but the robber cannot hold
that steady, agonized gaze.
Soon he realizes this man is in far more
pain than he, and he doesn't know why.
He flinches away, ashamed of himself
for ridiculing a weaker man.
But still he watches. In time, he realizes he's
never seen someone take execution like this,
and he's seen plenty.
He's never known a man to forgive his executioners,
but with this Man it sounded sincere.
Real. Holy.
He thinks about it.
Yes, holy.
He wants to forget everything,
just to die and be forgotten.
But in less than an hour, he's won over.
This Person is no mere man.

God Is!

He listens to the crowd and learns of
the things this man has done, what
words of hope He gave to His followers,
how He healed and comforted.
He concludes this man is indeed the
long-awaited King, the Jews' Messiah.
Somewhere deep inside him, something stirs.
A saying from his childhood,
something the rabbis said.
"He was a man of sorrows,
acquainted with grief . . .
He was despised and forsaken of men . . .
He was crushed for our iniquities . . .
All of us like sheep have gone astray,
but He has borne the iniquity of us all . . ."
He pauses on those last words and gasps. Suddenly, his
mind is filled with a supernatural comprehension,
as if a candle has flickered on in his heart.
He looks up into the man's face,

God Is!

the first pang of hope filling his breast.
As their eyes meet,
he suddenly remembers how
he has insulted Him. Reviled Him.
Joked with the crowd about Him.
He realizes he deserves the worst hell can
throw at him.
He turns away, despair gripping him like a rope
around his neck. He can't breathe.
He can't think.
Now he doesn't want to die.
A fear grabs him in the chest and won't let go.
It's pressing down upon him, a weight,
sinking him into hell.
Then somehow he looks up.
Jesus is gazing at him.
And in those eyes he sees something,
a warmth, a kindness — no, more: a love,
a love that demands no conditions,

God Is!

a love that can never cease or die.
He finally rasps, his throat tearing
with thirst and dryness,
"Jesus, remember me when you come
into your kingdom."
He doesn't want much.
Not a place. Not a position.
Not a title. He'll take whatever Jesus can give.
Jesus looks into his eyes and speaks.
"Today you will be with Me in Paradise."
As Jesus' eyes hold him, the thief realizes
some eternal transaction has just taken place, and
he has nothing to fear, ever again.
He swallows and nods, and then watches Jesus die, crying,
"Father, into Thy hands I commit My spirit."
Somewhere deep inside the robber realizes that
this execution was no ordinary death,
that this Man deserved none of this
but had gone to the cross willingly, gladly,

God Is!

so He could make possible the Paradise
that He had just promised him
The thief settles down on the nail binding
his feet to the cross and he whispers,
"Jesus, into Your hands I commit my spirit."
Some call it the first "foxhole conversion."
We call him "the thief on the cross."
God calls him the ultimate
"object of grace."

For by grace you have been saved
through faith;
and that not of yourselves,
it is the gift of God;
not as a result of works,
that no one should boast.

—Ephesians 2:8-9 NASB

Other Books by Starburst Publishers
(Partial listing—full list available on request)

God's Vitamin "C" for the Spirit — Kathy Collard Miller & D. Larry Miller

Subtitled: "Tug-at-the-Heart" Stories to Fortify and Enrich Your Life. Includes inspiring stories and anecdotes that emphasize Christian ideals and values by Barbara Johnson, Billy Graham, Patsy Clairmont, Max Lucado, James Dobson, Jack Hayford and many other well-known Christian speakers and writers. Topics include: Love, Family Life, Faith and Trust, Prayer, Marriage, Relationships, Grief, Spiritual Life, Perseverance, Christian Living, and God's Guidance.

(trade paper) ISBN 0914984837 **$12.95**

God's Chewable Vitamin "C" for the Spirit

A collection of inspirational Quotes and Scriptures by many of your favorite Christian speakers and writers.

(trade paper) ISBN 0914984845 **$6.95**

God's Vitamin "C" for the Spirit of WOMEN — Kathy Collard Miller

Subtitled: "Tug-at-the Heart" stories to Inspire and Delight Your Spirit. A beautiful treasury of timeless stories, quotes and poetry designed by and for women. Well-known Christian women like Liz Curtis Higgs, Pasty Clairmont, Naomi Rhode, Elisabeth Elliott share from their hearts on subjects like Marriage, Motherhood, Christian Living, Faith and Friendship.

(trade paper) ISBN 0914984934 **$12.95**

God's Chewable Vitamin "C" for the Spirit of MOMs

Delightful, Insightful and Inspirational quotes combined with Scriptures that uplift and encourage women to succeed at the most important job in life — Motherhood.

(trade paper) ISBN 0914984942 **$6.95**

God's Vitamin "C" for the Spirit of MEN — D. Larry Miller

Subtitled: "Tug-at-the-Heart" Stories to Encourage and Strengthen Your Spirit. Compiled in the format of best-selling God's Vitamin "C" for the Spirit, this book is filled with unique and inspiring stories that men of all ages will immediately relate to. True stories by some of the most-loved Christian speakers and writers on topics such as Integrity, Mentoring, Leadership, Marriage, Success/Failure, Family, Godliness, and Spiritual Life are sure to encourage men through the challenges of life. Contributors include Bill McCartney, Tony Evans, Larry Crabb, and R. C. Sproul, to name a few.

(trade paper) ISBN 0914984810 **$12.95**

God's Chewable Vitamin "C" for the Spirit of DADs

Scriptures coupled with insightful quotes to inspire men through the changes of life. This little "portable" is the perfect gift for men of all ages.

(trade paper) ISBN 0914984829 **$6.95**

Baby Steps to Happiness
—John Q. Baucom

Subtitled: 52 Inspiring Ways to Make Your Life Happy. This unique 52-step approach will enable the reader to focus on small steps that bring practical and proven change. Chapter titles, such as, Have a Reason to Get Out of Bed, Deal with Your Feelings or Become Them, give insight and encouragement on the road to happiness.

(trade paper) ISBN 0914984861 **$12.95**

Little Baby Steps to Happiness

Inspiring, witty and insightful, this portable collection of quotes and affirmations from Baby Steps to Happiness will encourage Happiness one little footstep at a time.

(trade paper) ISBN 091498487X **$6.95**

A Woman's Guide To Spiritual Power
—Nancy L. Dorner

Subtitled: Through Scriptural Prayer. Do your prayers seem to go "against a brick wall?" Does God sometimes seem far away or non-existent? If your answer is "Yes," You are not alone. Prayer must be the cornerstone of your relationship to God.

(trade paper) ISBN 0914984470 **$9.95**

From Grandma With Love
—Ann Tuites

Subtitled: Thoughts for Her Children Everywhere. People are taught all kinds of things from pre-school to graduate school, but they are expected to know how to get along with their families. Practical, emotional and spiritual support is given so that all generations can live together in harmony.

(hardcover) ISBN 0914984616 **$14.95**

Purchasing Information:

Listed books are available from your favorite Bookstore, either from current stock or special order. To assist bookstores in locating your selection be sure to give title, author, and ISBN #. If unable to purchase from the bookstore you may order direct from STARBURST PUBLISHERS. When ordering, enclose full payment plus $3.00 for shipping and handling ($4.00 if Canada or Overseas). Payment in US Funds only. Please allow two to three weeks minimum (longer overseas) for delivery. Make checks payable to and mail to STARBURST PUBLISHERS, P.O. Box 4123, LANCASTER, PA 17604. Prices subject to change without notice. Catalog available for a 9 x 12 self-addressed envelope with 4 first-class stamps.